writing guides

ACTIVITIES FOR WRITING

Soap

STORIES

GUY MERCHANT

LIVERPOOL
JOHN MOORES UNIVERSITY
I.M. MARSH LIBRARY
BARKHILL ROAD
LIVERPOOL L17 6BD
TEL. 0151 231 5216/5299

WITHDRAWN

FICTION
FOR AGES
7-9

D1151036

LIVERPOOL JMU LIBRARY

3 1111 01001 7638

Published by Scholastic Ltd,
Villiers House,
Clarendon Avenue,
Leamington Spa,
Warwickshire CV32 5PR
Designed using Adobe Pagemaker
Printed by Unwin
Brothers Ltd, Woking

© 2001 Scholastic Ltd
Text © Guy Merchant 2001

SERIES EDITOR
Huw Thomas

AUTHOR
Guy Merchant

EDITOR
Clare Gallaher

ASSISTANT EDITOR
Dulcie Booth

SERIES DESIGNER
Anna Oliwa

DESIGNER
Anna Oliwa

COVER ILLUSTRATION
Mark Oliver

ILLUSTRATIONS
Peter Stevenson

1 2 3 4 5 6 7 8 9 0   1 2 3 4 5 6 7 8 9 0

The publishers wish to thank:
HarperCollins Publishers Ltd
for the use of 'The Summer Night'
from *The Martian Chronicles* by
Ray Bradbury © 1995, Ray
Bradbury (1994, HarperCollins).
Rogers Coleridge and White for
the use of 'Skyjacked' by Mary
Hoffman from *Fantastic Space
Stories* edited by Tony Bradman
© 1995, Mary Hoffman
(1995, Corgi Books).

Every effort has been made to
trace copyright holders and the
publishers apologise for any
omissions.

Thanks to the pupils and staff of
Our Lady's and St Joseph's
Primary School, Wath-upon-
Dearne.

British Library Cataloguing-in-Publication Data
A catalogue record for this book is available from the
British Library.

ISBN 0-439-01869-2

The right of Guy Merchant to be identified as the Author
of this work has been asserted by him in accordance
with the Copyright, Designs and Patents Act 1988.

All rights reserved. This book is sold subject to the
condition that it shall not, by way of trade or otherwise,
be lent, hired out or otherwise circulated without the
publisher's prior consent in any form of binding or cover
other than that in which it is published and without a
similar condition, including this condition, being
imposed upon the subsequent purchaser.

No part of this publication may be reproduced, stored
in a retrieval system, or transmitted, in any form or by
any means, electronic, mechanical, photocopying,
recording or otherwise, without the prior permission of
the publisher. This book remains copyright, although
permission is granted to copy those pages indicated as
photocopiable for classroom distribution and use only
in the school which has purchased the book, or by the
teacher who has purchased the book, and in accordance
with the CLA licensing agreement. Photocopying
permission is given for purchasers only and not for
borrowers of books from any lending service.

CONTENTS

Skyjacked

Trel looked up from the console and stretched her shoulders till they cracked. It had been a long day. First navigating the meteor shower, then dealing with a laser rocket attack while half the ship's defence systems were down, and finally the last manoeuvre to avoid being sucked into a black hole. She flexed her fingers and glanced back up at the viewscreen. "What now?" A row of brilliant white fire-flashes was approaching. "Disintegrating ship? Comet? Kamikaze attack?"

The doors to the flight deck swooshed open and a sandy-haired boy a bit older than Trel burst in.

"Message from Commander Arcturus," he barked.

from 'Skyjacked' by Mary Hoffman in
Fantastic Space Stories

The summer night

In the stone galleries the people were gathered in clusters and groups filtering up into shadows among the blue hills. A soft evening light shone over them from the stars and the luminous double moons of Mars. Beyond the marble amphitheatre, in darknesses and distances, lay little towns and villas; pools of silver water stood motionless and canals glittered from horizon to horizon. It was an evening in summer upon the placid and temperate planet Mars. Up and down green wine-canals, boats as delicate as bronze flowers drifted. In the long and endless dwellings that curved like tranquil snakes across the hills, lovers lay idly whispering in cool night beds. The last children ran in torchlit alleys, gold spiders in their hands throwing out films of web. Here or there a late supper was prepared in tables where lava bubbled silvery and hushed. In the amphitheatre of a hundred towns on the night side of Mars the brown Martian people with gold coin eyes were leisurely met to fix their attention upon stages where musicians made a serene music flow up like blossom scent on the still air.

from *The Martian Chronicles* by Ray Bradbury

 I.M. MARSH LIBRARY LIVERPOOL L17 6BD
TEL. 0151 231 5216/5299

Out in space: on the bridge

How do you know that 'Skyjacked' is a science fiction story? Use the columns to keep a record.

WHAT CAN YOU SEE?

WHAT WORDS ARE USED?

WHAT'S GOING ON?

CHARACTER NAMES:

writing guides: **SCI-FI STORIES**

Being there: on another planet

A science fiction writer often needs to create an imaginary scene.
Ray Bradbury is painting a picture of Mars with words.

Sci-fi (science fiction) is, as its name suggests, fiction that describes events that might really happen if scientific speculation became reality. Unlike fantasy writing, sci-fi is based on scientific fact and possibility. Sci-fi writing often transports the reader to an imaginary future time in which technological innovation makes the extraordinary possible. Sophisticated computers and robots are common; travel to other galaxies and encounters with alien life forms are always likely. Problems are solved by scientific or technological means and human characters usually behave in quite predictable ways. For children, sci-fi writing is ideal for extending the imagination and for working creatively with writing technique as they describe imaginary characters and events that take place in unusual settings.

Shared activities

'Skyjacked' extract

This is the opening of a short story by Mary Hoffman in *Fantastic Space Stories*, edited by Tony Bradman (Corgi Books), which quickly creates the sense of computer-based navigation through space. It introduces a spaceship setting through the use of technical vocabulary. The illustration, title and character names all suggest the sci-fi genre. Trel is navigating through deep space… or is she?

After reading the extract on page 4 with the children in a shared reading session, ask them where they think it is set. Do they know what kind of writing it is? (Introduce the term *science fiction*.) Talk about why the story is called 'Skyjacked'; what might happen next? Discuss what other things might happen in a sci-fi story.

The Martian Chronicles extract

Ray Bradbury wrote *The Martian Chronicles* in 1951 when space travel was in its infancy. In this extract he depicts what it might be like to live in a human settlement on Mars. He creates an image of a dreamy, relaxed way of life which contrasts with the homesickness of the human settlers.

As you read page 5 with the children, ask them to identify unusual or unfamiliar vocabulary, to be discussed afterwards. Talk about the *brown Martian people with gold coin eyes*: are they humans or are they alien beings? What sort of 'people' do the children think they are? Focus on the setting and discuss the mood Bradbury creates.

Out in space: on the bridge

Display an enlarged copy (or OHT) of photocopiable page 4. Ask the children how they can tell that the extract is from a sci-fi story. Discuss their ideas, recording them on a displayed copy of photocopiable page 6. Draw the children's attention to the 'technical' vocabulary (*comet, console*, and so on).

Being there: on another planet

Display an enlarged copy (or OHT) of photocopiable page 5. Re-read the extract, then ask the children what sort of place they imagined. Is it friendly, dangerous or just unusual? Identify objects and people (nouns) and how they are described (adjectives). Write these on Post-it Notes (for example, *stone galleries; luminous double moons*). Display a copy of photocopiable page 7, asking the children to help you decide where to place the Post-it Notes – on or above the surface of the planet. Conclude this session by talking with the children about the 'mood' of the extract. How is the relaxed, dreamy feeling created? Jot down the children's ideas on the bottom half of the photocopiable sheet. Note that the mood is created by verbs (*filtering, glittered, drifted*) and similes (*like tranquil snakes*) as well as adjectives.

writing guides: **SCI-FI STORIES**

Sci-fi ideas: a writer's notebook

Writers often keep notebooks of ideas that they might use in stories. Start your notebook on the two pages below. Jot down words and phrases under each heading.

On a distant planet

What it looks like

Buildings

What's going on?

Travelling through space

Kind of spaceship

Things inside

Things outside

I.M. MARSH LIBRARY LIVERPOOL L17 6BD
TEL. 0151 231 5216/5299

MAKING SCIENCE FICTION

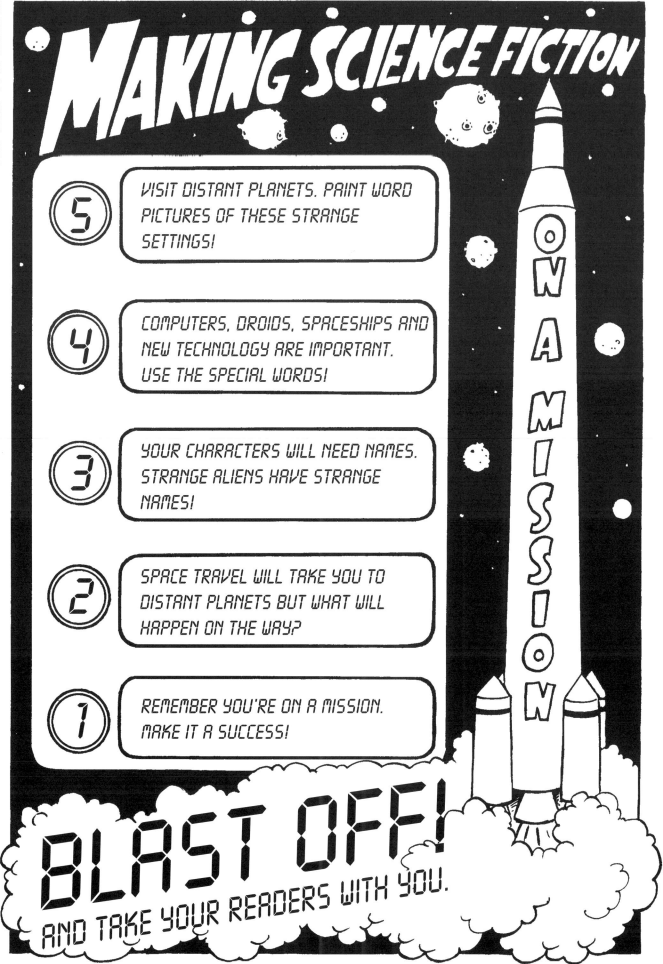

5 VISIT DISTANT PLANETS. PAINT WORD PICTURES OF THESE STRANGE SETTINGS!

4 COMPUTERS, DROIDS, SPACESHIPS AND NEW TECHNOLOGY ARE IMPORTANT. USE THE SPECIAL WORDS!

3 YOUR CHARACTERS WILL NEED NAMES. STRANGE ALIENS HAVE STRANGE NAMES!

2 SPACE TRAVEL WILL TAKE YOU TO DISTANT PLANETS BUT WHAT WILL HAPPEN ON THE WAY?

1 REMEMBER YOU'RE ON A MISSION. MAKE IT A SUCCESS!

ON A MISSION

BLAST OFF!
AND TAKE YOUR READERS WITH YOU.

writing guides: **SCI-FI STORIES**

Taking ideas further

So far, Section One has helped you to identify some important features of sci-fi writing. Many children will have a rich experience of these kinds of stories from television, video and film and it is important to draw on this experience. You will find it useful to look at a short extract from something like *The Phantom Menace* (Star Wars – Episode 1), which will give more clues about the sci-fi genre, such as the importance of setting and the use of technological innovation. However, translating these sorts of narratives into the written form can be quite challenging. The first two activities introduced practical approaches, aimed at helping children to learn how to 'paint a picture with words'.

Sci-fi ideas: a writer's notebook

The activity on photocopiable page 9 introduces the idea of keeping a writer's notebook (or scrapbook). Many professional writers do this and it is very useful to get children to experiment with the technique. It shows them that they can collect ideas as they go along, deciding whether or not to use and develop them at a later date. Scrapbooks can also be used to collect pictures of popular sci-fi characters and children's own sketches. Sometimes you can also tie in work done in other subjects such as science, technology or art.

Making science fiction

Photocopiable page 10 draws together some of the main features of sci-fi writing and is a guide that can be referred to throughout the project. You can either enlarge it to make a poster for the classroom wall or provide children with individual copies for their writer's notebooks. This can be used to remind them of what they have learned.

Extension ideas

● It is always useful to extend children's knowledge of a particular style of writing with more examples. Used as a class novel or for independent reading try *Fantastic Space Stories* by Tony Bradman (Corgi) or *Haddock 'n' Chips* by Linda Hoy (Walker Books). Colin McNaughton's *Here Come the Aliens!* (Walker Books) is a good example of a sci-fi picture book and *Jo-Jo's Journey* by Grahame Barker-Smith (Bodley Head) introduces the comic book genre.

● Three-dimensional modelling is also a useful way for children to explore setting and you can do this by creating table-top displays or 'small worlds' in an old shoebox. Models or Lego people can be used to bring these to life. As children read up on how writers and film directors develop a sci-fi world they will understand the importance of modelling and sketching in supporting the writing process.

● There are some lavishly illustrated film tie-in books from the makers of *Star Wars* and *Star Trek* which could help children to connect with this writing project. They will also find it useful to look at some factual sources. *Space News* by Michael Johnstone and Douglas Millard (Walker Books) is particularly good on the history of space travel. Clive Gifford's *How to Live on Mars* (Oxford University Press) is amusing and has useful practical activities, whereas *Informania: Aliens* by Jacqueline Mitton (Walker Books) will be useful for the inevitable alien encounter.

● Internet sites such as www.starwarskids.com and www.startrek.com are well worth a visit, as is http://kids.msfc.nasa.gov – the NASA site.

This section provides guidance on the first stages of the sci-fi writing process. This work can be an individual or a group project. Whichever you choose you will need to pay close attention to planning and organisation. In writing longer stories children need to develop a clear plot structure with key events. They will also have to make decisions about the sequence of events, where to provide the reader with additional detail and where this is not necessary. The activities in this section help children to reach these decisions. The first activity, 'Introducing the sci-fi story' (page 14), is an introduction to the writing project and will guide children's thoughts about purpose and audience as they recall some key characteristics of sci-fi that they have learned about in Section One.

What's the story?

The next three activities guide children through the process of planning the key events in their story. 'Mission possible: 1' (page 13) helps children to think through the reason for the space journey they are going to write about. Four prompts are given, but children should be encouraged to add their own. 'Mission possible: 2' (page 13) looks at how their story problem is solved and encourages children to think of a resolution that will make their mission a success. 'On a mission' (page 14) maps the overall shape of the story while giving children ideas about minor events that will add colour to the journey. The additional photocopiable activity 'Star trick' (page 14) helps children to build more detail around these minor events through writing a captain's log.

Who's in it?

'Meet the crew' (page 14) and 'Invent an alien' (page 15) are activities to encourage children to think about the characters that will appear in the story. In 'Meet the crew' they create the team of space travellers for their mission. Children may like to base these characters on themselves, although they will need to be imaginative about their looks and characteristics! 'Invent an alien' helps children to design and name a variety of alien creatures. These can be developed by creating casting notes like those in Mitton's *Informania: Aliens* or in *Star Wars Who's Who* by Ryder Windham (Running Press).

Where does it happen?

I suggest three main locations for the story – Earth, the spaceship, and another planet. Children will create these settings and describe them based on the writing models in Section One. 'Ground control' (page 15) is the headquarters on Earth and in this activity children will be experimenting with descriptive language to create the picture of a hi-tech base for the start and finish of the adventure. Designing the spaceship which transports the crew through space is supported by the activity 'Silver machine' (page 15). In 'Is their life on Mars?' (page 16) the children can think about how they are going to use factual research to inform their sci-fi writing. The final task, 'On your planet' (page 16), helps them to create an imaginary setting by constructing a map (or three-dimensional model) of their planet destination.

INTRODUCING THE SCI-FI STORY

WHAT YOU NEED

Board or flip chart, Post-it Notes, writing materials.

WHAT TO DO

Before you start this session write the aims of the project on the board: *To work on an exciting sci-fi adventure story for other children.* You may have already decided upon the audience (for example, children in another school, or a parallel age range in your own school) or you might want this to be part of your discussion.

Begin by explaining that the purpose of the activities they will be undertaking on sci-fi stories is to enable them to write their own. Remind the children how they will be drawing on what they have learned through the activities in Section One. Then ask the children to work in pairs. Give each pair five or six Post-it Notes and ask them to jot down things that their audience would like in a good sci-fi adventure. After a few minutes these can be put up on the board and discussed. At this point you can be reminding children about the key features of sci-fi writing that were introduced earlier. Conclude the session by explaining that their story (or stories) are going to be based on a journey from Earth to a distant planet.

OBJECTIVES

- To explain the process of writing a sci-fi story.
- To consider what readers of sci-fi stories expect.
- To understand the key features of good sci-fi writing

MISSION POSSIBLE: 1

WHAT YOU NEED

Photocopiable page 17, writing materials (including thick felt-tipped pens), plain A4 paper.

WHAT TO DO

Begin with a short discussion about problems and solutions in stories (you may well have covered this in previous text-level work). Have a few examples of your own, but encourage children to draw on their experience of story and film. Children who are familiar with *Star Wars* or *Star Trek* may have specific examples from the sci-fi genre. Others can draw on stories you have shared (such as *Haddock 'n' Chips*).

Remind children that their sci-fi story involves a journey to another planet and that the first step is to have a reason for this journey. Ask them to work in pairs to complete the 'Mission possible: 1' ideas sheet. On the reverse side of the activity sheet they can brainstorm three more problems or conflicts on Mars.

To extend and develop this work, ask the children to choose one of their 'Mission possible' ideas to draft a newspaper headline (for example, *CRISIS ON MARS: rescue mission to save scientist*). Explain that they are allowed a maximum of four upper-case words for the headline and five lower-case words for the subtitle.

OBJECTIVES

- To reflect on the overall structure of the sci-fi story.
- To identify specific problems or conflicts that will be resolved in the story.

MISSION POSSIBLE: 2

WHAT YOU NEED

Completed copies of photocopiable page 17, board or flip chart (or plain A4 paper folded into two), writing materials.

WHAT TO DO

Remind the children of the importance of having a good plot structure for their sci-fi story. Explain that you are going to focus on possible 'missions' and how they can be successful. If this is a whole-class activity, write two columns on the board, one headed *Possible missions* and the other *Successes*; if you are working in a group, you may want children to record this themselves on A4 paper.

OBJECTIVES

- To reflect on the overall structure of the sci-fi story.
- To identify resolutions to the problems or conflicts in the sci-fi story.

writing guides: **SCI-FI STORIES**

LIVERPOOL JOHN MOORES UNIVERSITY
LEARNING & INFORMATION SERVICES

Go through the children's responses to 'Mission impossible: 1'. Write these in the *Possible missions* column. Then discuss how the problems could be solved, or how a journey to another planet could lead to success.

Extend and develop these ideas by working with the children to draft a short paragraph that explains the solution to one of the problems. This can be done as guided writing. Children should read back their draft paragraphs and discuss their effectiveness.

ON A MISSION

WHAT YOU NEED

Photocopiable page 18, black backing paper, scraps of brightly coloured paper, scissors, glitter, glue, writing materials.

WHAT TO DO

This activity will help children to reach some decisions about the mission they are planning and also the minor incidents or sub-plots that will be part of the build-up (refer back to the 'Skyjacked' extract in Section One). These sub-plots can be explained as delays or events to keep the reader interested during the space journey.

Read the activity sheet with the children. They can then trace the route and cut and paste incidents or jot down ideas of their own.

Extend and develop this activity by providing large sheets of black backing paper, brighter scraps (for stars and planets), glitter and glue. The children can then paste notes on this plan that will remind them of the sequence of events, the main 'mission' and the minor incidents.

STAR TRICK

WHAT YOU NEED

Photocopiable page 19, writing materials, tape recorder.

WHAT TO DO

This activity helps children to develop some of the minor incidents and to experiment with the journal form of writing, which they may choose to incorporate in their final piece.

Begin by modelling the journal form of writing based on a minor incident of your own. This may be based on the captain's log from *Star Trek*. Now ask the children to work individually or in pairs to develop their own captain's log on the activity sheet. This can be used as a script for an audio-taped version, as an extension activity.

MEET THE CREW

WHAT YOU NEED

Photocopiable page 20, writing materials.

WHAT TO DO

Start this activity by modelling a character description, using the same format as the photocopiable sheet. Use the same titles (*name, job, appearance, personality*). A colour photograph from a magazine could be used to prompt children's imagination. Use the 'job' category to think about the character's role on the journey (captain, doctor, engineer, scientist, and so on). Encourage the children to think carefully about the adjectives they will use to paint a verbal picture of crew members. Model

OBJECTIVES

■ To plan the overall shape of the sci-fi story.
■ To begin to consider sub-plots or incidental events.

OBJECTIVES

■ To develop sub-plots or incidental events in sci-fi writing.
■ To sequence events within a sub-plot.
■ To write sci-fi episodes in journal form.

OBJECTIVES

■ To develop characters for a journey to another planet.
■ To think of the different personalities of crew members.
■ To apply knowledge of similes and adjectives in character description.

the use of similes in your own description of personality (the captain could be *as steady as a rock*; the scientist might have *a brain like a suite of computers*). Personalities could have strengths and weaknesses!

Children can now create their own crew, using the activity sheet. One of the character cards has a large star. This character is a 'wild card', and children can build in some surprise or hidden aspect to this character (for example, he or she is really a 'baddie', or looks human but is really an alien). As an extension activity, children can read each other's character cards. They can then go into role as these characters, while other children ask them questions in a hot-seating exercise.

INVENT AN ALIEN

WHAT YOU NEED

A4 paper folded into three, writing materials.

WHAT TO DO

This activity is a variant of the game of consequences and is a useful device for creating imaginary characters. Explain the procedure first, reminding the children that each stage is private. The first child draws an alien head (or heads) ending in a neck at the first fold. The two neck lines should run just over the fold so that the second child can draw the body. Make sure that the drawing of the head is folded back so that the second child cannot see it. Repeat this process, leaving lines for legs but remembering to fold the paper so the body isn't visible. The third child then opens the picture up. Children can then work individually to give their alien a name and to draft 'casting notes'.

OBJECTIVES

■ To design an alien character.

■ To use descriptive language in writing 'casting notes' for an alien character.

GROUND CONTROL

WHAT YOU NEED

Board or flip chart, writing materials.

WHAT TO DO

Explain to the children that their sci-fi adventure takes place in the year 2525. Get them to calculate how far in the future that is. Ask them to imagine what a space control centre might be like in 500 years time. If you can find some pictures of NASA this could be used as a trigger – otherwise visit their website (www.nasa.gov). Write notes on what children say about ground control on the board. Use these notes to model a descriptive piece about ground control.

Develop the activity by asking children to write their own descriptive passages. These will be refined and used in their story.

OBJECTIVES

■ To brainstorm a description of an initial setting – a space control centre.

■ To use descriptive language to describe the initial setting.

■ To develop writing from notes.

SILVER MACHINE

WHAT YOU NEED

A labelled diagram showing a cross-section (for example, a diagram of a car or aircraft), photocopiable page 21, writing materials.

WHAT TO DO

Introduce the task by talking about how a cross-section represents an X-ray view of an object. Explain how a key can refer you to specific areas. *Star Wars* tie-in books are particularly useful to model this exercise. Discuss the activity sheet and demonstrate how to use the key. Children can now work in pairs or small groups to

OBJECTIVES

■ To develop ideas for sci-fi settings.

■ To make notes and label a diagram of a spaceship.

■ To use instructional language.

fill in the detail and decide on the labels. Explain that when they have completed this they are going to write instructions for navigating their spaceship. They can do this on the back of the sheet. They may need to go back to the cross-section to introduce new equipment (for example, joysticks, booster rockets...).

Extend this activity by helping the children to use their plans to build a model spaceship for a technology project.

IS THERE LIFE ON MARS?

WHAT YOU NEED
Photocopiable page 22, board or flip chart, writing materials, A4 paper.

OBJECTIVE
■ To use factual research to inform sci-fi writing.

WHAT TO DO
Explain how sci-fi writers will often do research to provide them with basic factual information before they let their imagination take over. Provide the children with copies of the photocopiable sheet. Look at the first statement (*It would take an astronaut about 6 months to reach Mars.*). Ask the children how they might use this fact. For example, they might say that they would use that timescale for the 'outward' journey of their story. Or they might say they would create a problem that would prolong the journey and put astronauts' lives in danger. Write a few of their ideas for the first statement on the board.

Ask the children to work in pairs to make notes about how they might use the facts on the sheet. Remind them that they can always ignore some facts in their story; they don't have to use every single fact they find! So their notes might read something like this: *very cold; will need special clothing; no oxygen – let's ignore this; large channels may be useful for landing in; Mariner Valley – good place for a space station.*

To extend and develop this activity, children can turn their notes into short statements to be used later when writing their stories.

ON YOUR PLANET

WHAT YOU NEED
Large sheets of paper (A1 size), location cards (include some blank cards).

OBJECTIVES
■ To develop further ideas on sci-fi setting.
■ To use descriptive and figurative language to evoke an imaginary landscape.

WHAT TO DO
Explain to the children that they will be designing their final setting by drawing a map of their planet. Prepare for this activity by making some labels (for example, *extremely steep valley, climate control centre, dark labyrinth of caves, uneven landing strip, underground city, giant volcano, rocky desert, abandoned mineral mines, space station*). Also have some blank cards available, so that the children can make their own labels drawn from the previous activity, 'Is there life on Mars?'.

Ask the children to work in pairs to map out the buildings and landforms of their planet. Encourage them to move the labels around until they reach a decision about what goes where. Simple sketches (or symbols) can be used and the labels can be stuck down to identify key features.

writing guides: **SCI-FI STORIES**

Mission possible: 1

A sci-fi story often has a journey through space and a mission to solve a problem. Read the starters in each asteroid and work with a friend to complete the sentence.

Aliens from an unknown galaxy have invaded Planet Alpha 2 and

A scientist on a Federation space station is in trouble. She is

Computer failure at the Nor Spacelab has caused

Unusually high temperatures are making life very difficult for human settlers on Mars and they

On a mission

Map your journey and think about things that happen on the way.
Cut out the words at the bottom of the sheet, paste them onto the
map or use your own ideas.

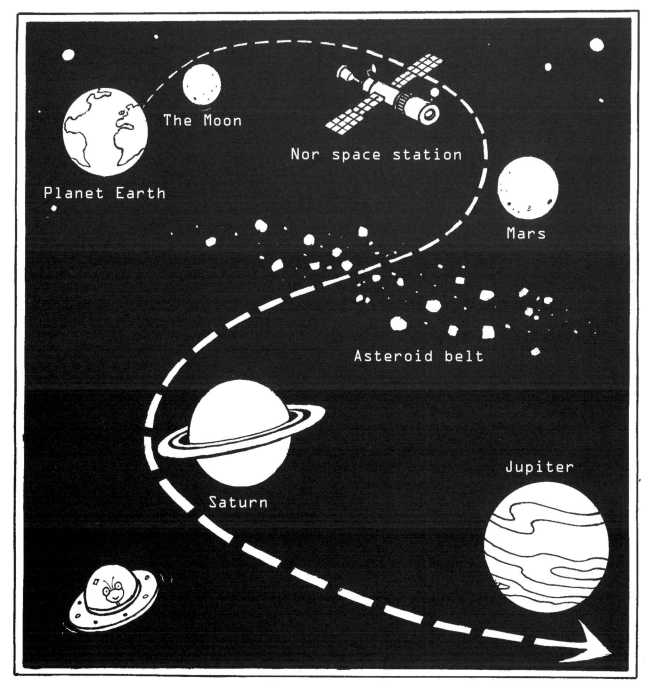

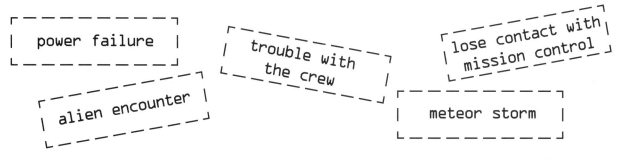

power failure

trouble with
the crew

lose contact with
mission control

alien encounter

meteor storm

writing guides: **SCI-FI STORIES**

Star trick

Some things go wrong on your space journey. Think of one event to write about. Use the captain's log to fill in the detail of that event.

CAPTAIN'S LOG DATE: 15:2:2525
OUR MISSION IS

CAPTAIN'S LOG DATE: 29:2:2525
SOMETHING STRANGE HAS HAPPENED

CAPTAIN'S LOG DATE: 17:2:2525
TAKE-OFF WAS

CAPTAIN'S LOG DATE: 2:3:2525
WE'RE ALL GLAD TO BE ALIVE

CAPTAIN'S LOG DATE: 27:2:2525
AFTER 10 DAYS IN SPACE THE CREW

CAPTAIN'S LOG DATE: 10:4:2525
WE ARE DUE TO LAND ON

Meet the crew

Use the boxes below to create character cards for
your crew – don't forget to use descriptive words.
One of the character cards has a star on it.
This character cannot be trusted. Why?

Name:

Job:

Appearance:

Personality:

Name:

Job:

Appearance:

Personality:

Name:

Job:

Appearance:

Personality:

Name:

Job:

Appearance:

Personality:

Silver machine

Work together to design your own spaceship. Finish the cross-section and label it with numbers. Use the key to describe different parts of the spaceship.

Plan of the spaceship

Key		
1	2	3
4	5	6

Write instructions for starting, controlling and navigating your spaceship, on the other side of this sheet.

I.M. MARSH LIBRARY LIVERPOOL L17 6BD
TEL. 0151 231 5216/5299

Is there life on Mars?

Make notes about how you might use these facts for your sci-fi story.

Facts	Notes
It would take an astronaut about 6 months to reach Mars.	
Mars has no liquid water and no plant life.	
Mars can be extremely cold (-23°C).	
There is no oxygen on Mars.	
There are large channels on Mars probably formed by water long ago.	
Mars is red in colour. It is often called **the red planet.**	
There is less gravity on Mars – objects would seem lighter.	
The surface of Mars is like a desert.	
The surface is mostly iron oxide (rust). This is why it has a red colour.	
There is an enormous volcano on Mars.	
There is a massive valley called Mariner Valley.	

writing guides: **SCI-FI STORIES**

This section helps you to develop the children's writing from the ideas planned in Section Two. The activities are designed so that children focus on one aspect of their sci-fi story. They deal with setting, character and with problems and solutions. If the children are organising their writing in chapters, these pieces of writing will play an important role in giving individual chapters a focus.

Before starting this section it will be useful for children to finalise their story plan. This is important whether they are working individually or collaboratively. The activities in Section Two will have generated plenty of material. Get the children to organise their story into six parts (or chapters). Do this by drawing a grid on a large sheet of paper. The children can jot down notes, make sketches or pin activity sheets from Section One onto the grid. For example, part 3 might be titled Getting there *and would include details of the spaceship setting from the activity 'Silver machine' (page 15) and some minor incidents from the activity 'Star trick' (page 14).*

On location: sci-fi places

The children can use the double-page spread on photocopiable pages 24 and 25 to work in groups to write two descriptions: one of the spaceship and the other of an alien landscape. They will need to have to hand supporting activity sheets that they have completed, such as 'Sci-fi ideas: a writer's notebook' (page 9) and 'Silver machine' (page 21), and their ideas from previous activities such as 'Invent an alien' (page 15) and 'Ground control' (page 15), together with any sketches, magazine pictures or books they have collected. You may need to remind them that this is time to write, not to research. That stage should now have been completed.

First they need to cut out the questions – make sure they understand that one set relates to the spaceship and the other one to the alien landscape. Which are the most important questions to write about? How can they extend their descriptions? They can then paste the questions they have chosen onto another sheet of paper and write in response to them. Encourage them to use imaginative adjectives and similes.

Sci-fi characters: crew members and aliens

The double-page spread on photocopiable pages 26 and 27 provides a framework for descriptions of crew members and aliens. As with the previous activity, the children will need supporting materials to hand. For example, their completed activity sheets 'Meet the crew' (page 20) can be used for reference when providing a more detailed analysis of the characters here.

Mission: what's the point?

The children can write about the central problem or point of their story, using the double-page spread on photocopiable pages 28 and 29 as a prompt sheet. As with the previous activities, they will need supporting materials to hand, such as their completed sheets for 'Mission possible: 1' (page 17), 'Mission possible: 2' (page 13) and 'On a mission' (page 18). Children will need to work hard to build excitement into this piece of writing. It needs to be fairly dramatic – whether it's a battle or a difficult task to be completed in a short time, for example. Encourage the children to spend additional time redrafting their writing after they have had feedback from other children and adults. They may wish to add their own questions or prompts to the sheets.

On location: sci-fi places

These two pages will help you to work on your description of settings.
Cut out the important questions to help you.

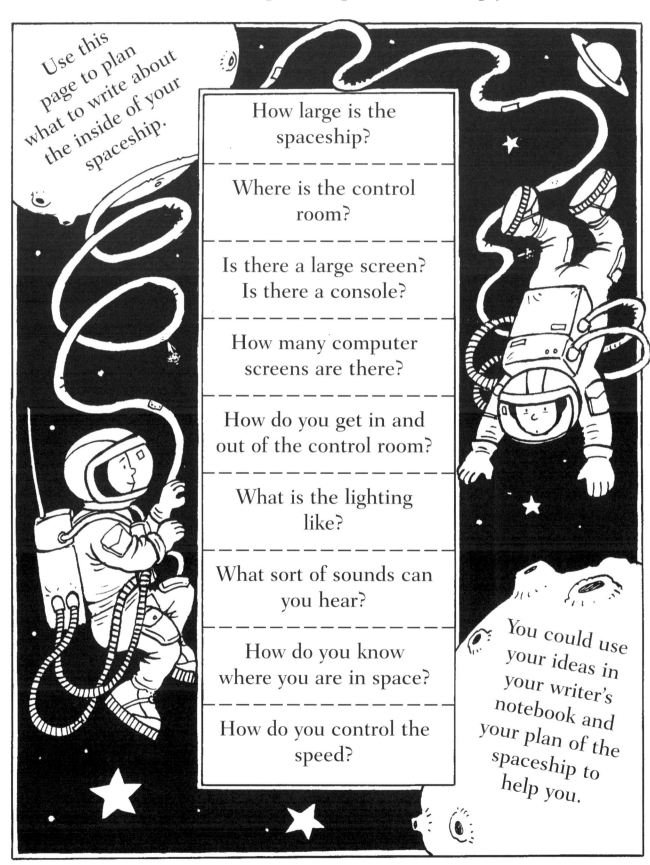

Use this page to plan what to write about the inside of your spaceship.

How large is the spaceship?

Where is the control room?

Is there a large screen? Is there a console?

How many computer screens are there?

How do you get in and out of the control room?

What is the lighting like?

What sort of sounds can you hear?

How do you know where you are in space?

How do you control the speed?

You could use your ideas in your writer's notebook and your plan of the spaceship to help you.

writing guides: **SCI-FI STORIES**

On location: sci-fi places

Use this page to describe what you see when your crew first sets foot on another planet.

Where are you?	Is there any sign of life?
What is the ground like?	Are there any buildings?
What can you see?	Is anything moving?
Is it warm or cold?	How easy is it to move?
Do you feel safe?	What direction are you travelling in?
Can you hear anything?	What sort of landforms can you see?

You could use your writer's notebook and your ideas for an alien character and a space control centre to help you.

I.M. MARSH LIBRARY LIVERPOOL L17 6BD
TEL. 0151 231 5216/5299

Sci-fi characters: crew members

Write descriptions of two crew members. These will become part of your final story. Draw small portraits to match your descriptions.

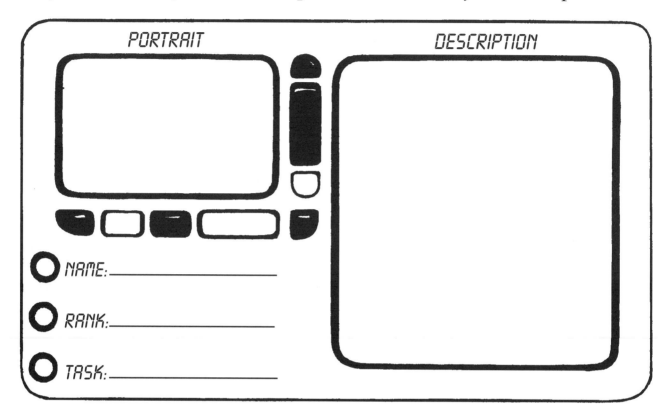

WHAT DO THEIR FACES LOOK LIKE? HOW BIG ARE THEY? WHAT ARE THEIR BODIES LIKE? WHAT ARE THEY WEARING? HOW DO THEY MOVE? HOW DO THEY SPEAK?

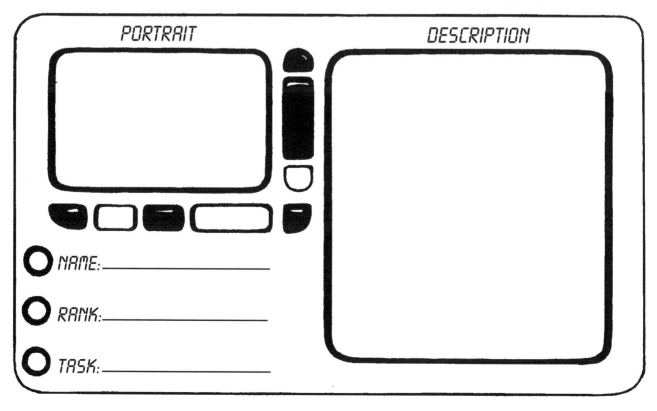

Sci-fi characters: aliens

Write descriptions of two aliens. These will become part of your final story. Draw small portraits to match your descriptions.

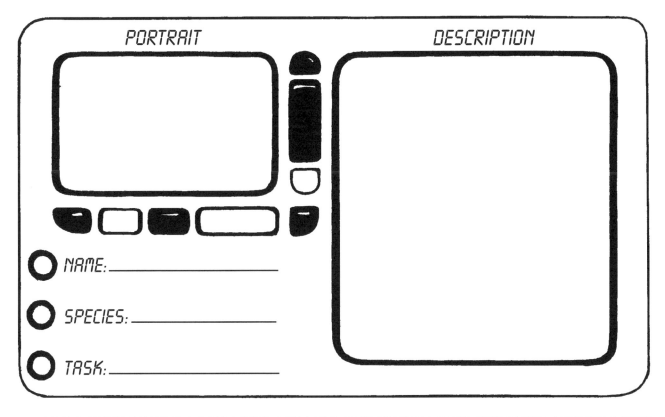

PORTRAIT

DESCRIPTION

NAME: _____

SPECIES: _____

TASK: _____

WHAT DO THEIR FACES LOOK LIKE? HOW BIG ARE THEY? WHAT ARE THEIR BODIES LIKE?
WHAT ARE THEY WEARING? HOW DO THEY MOVE? HOW DO THEY SPEAK?

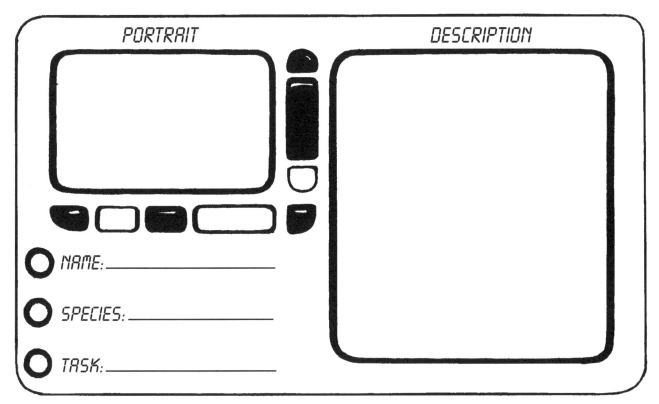

PORTRAIT

DESCRIPTION

NAME: _____

SPECIES: _____

TASK: _____

Mission: what's the point?

Describe the exciting central point of your story.
This is the point at which your mission becomes a success.
Use these pages to sort out your ideas.

writing guides: **SCI-FI STORIES**

Mission: what's the point?

This section provides guidance on helping children to identify what they have learned about sci-fi writing and to look at the strengths and weaknesses of the work they have produced. Two photocopiable activities guide this process of reflection. The final activity supports children in identifying targets to improve their writing in the future.

In your own assessment of children's work it will be important to evaluate their progress against a variety of objectives. In doing this you may want to look at what they have produced at various stages in the writing project as well as the final story itself. For instance, their work from activities in Section Two may well present good evidence of their achievement. If they have used a writer's notebook this will be useful in assessing their understanding of the writing process.

Sci-fi: what is it?

Before you start the activity on photocopiable page 31, talk to the children about what they have learned about sci-fi writing through working on this project. Explain that they are going to look at some statements and think about whether they could be used to describe sci-fi writing. You may want to provide some additional strips of paper so that they can write more statements of their own. The activity can be done individually or in pairs. Children can use their statements to evaluate the stories they have written and other sci-fi adventures they have read.

Sci-fi writing: mission report

The activity on photocopiable page 32 encourages children to review the stories that they have written and the particular writing techniques that they have developed. They can reflect on the writing process, style, plot, character and setting. The activity concludes with setting three targets; these could be restricted to the sci-fi genre or you may wish them to be more general in order to identify short-term writing targets.

Sci-fi: what is it?

Read the sentences, cut them out and stick them on a sheet of paper.
Put the most important sentence at the top.
If there's a sentence you don't agree with, turn it over and write your
own on the other side.

It's exciting – there's lots of action
and danger in it.

It seems real – you can see it because
it uses good descriptive language.

It's chewy – there's at least one
good recipe in it.

It works – something gets sorted out
and the story has a point.

It's scary – you could easily get
frightened.

It's strange – there's at least one
weird alien or droid in it.

It's magical – there are elves,
wizards and spells in it.

It makes you think – it could all
be possible in the future.

writing guides: **SCI-FI STORIES**

Sci-fi writing: mission report

You've just completed a mission to write a sci-fi story.
Use this mission report form to think about what you did.

MISSION REPORT   No495.7

Getting ideas about sci-fi
I got my ideas by:

1_____

2_____

3_____

4_____

Putting it into words
I created a sci-fi story
by using

_____

_____

_____

_____

Three ways I could improve
my writing

1_____

_____

2_____

_____

3_____

_____

The sci-fi story
The story was good sci-fi
because

_____

_____

It would be better if

_____

_____

People and places
My favourite crew member was

_____

because_____

_____

My favourite alien was

_____

because_____

My favourite setting was

_____

because_____

_____